The Nutcracker

Performed by

New York City Ballet

GEORGE BALANCHINE'S

The Nu

ELEKTRA ENTERTAINMENT   LITTLE, BROWN AND COMPANY

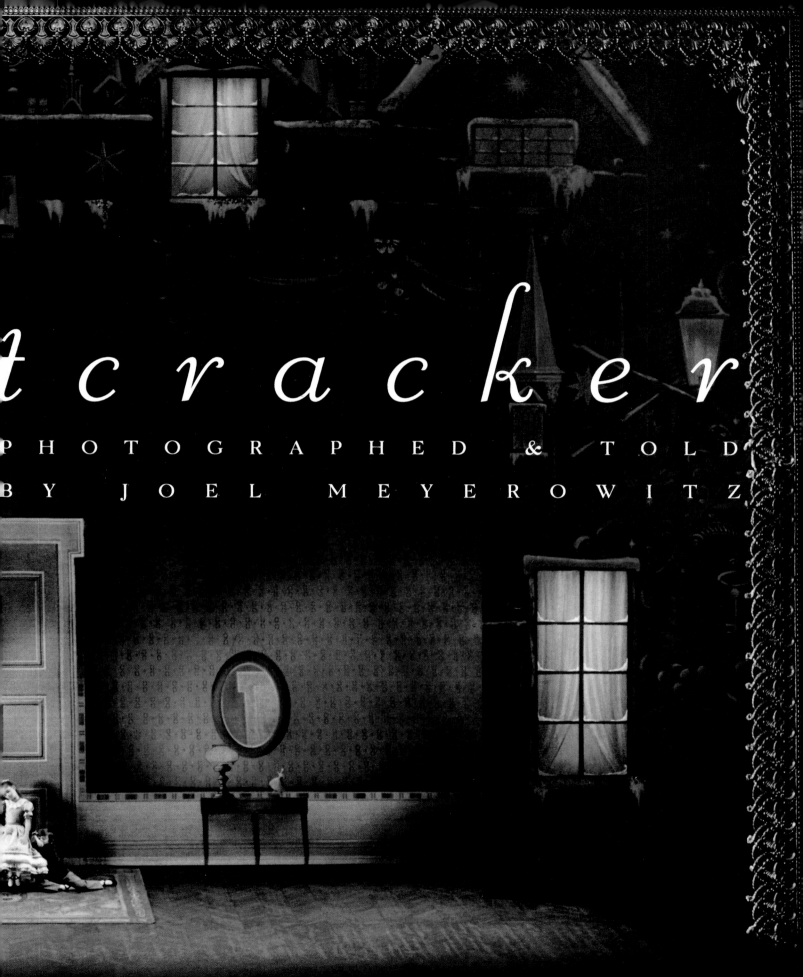

tcracker

PHOTOGRAPHED & TOLD
BY JOEL MEYEROWITZ

BOSTON·NEW YORK·TORONTO·LONDON   A FLOYD YEAROUT BOOK

IT WAS SNOWING ON CHRISTMAS EVE. Big flakes fell, swirling and glittering like dancers dressed in crystal costumes. Marie drifted in and out of a dream where she too was spinning like a snowflake. She and her brother, Fritz, were so excited about tonight's party they had to be asked many times to calm down. Finally Mama and Papa Stalhbaum closed the big living room doors and told the children for the last time, "Be patient, please!" and made them wait in the entrance parlor. Marie pulled a chair in front of the door, ready for the first moment they would be welcomed back into the living room. They sat there for so long trying to be good they finally became drowsy. Marie's last thought as she was nodding off was that if Fritz hadn't been such a devil today, as usual, they might still be in the living room with its sweet smells of hot chocolate and gingerbread, peppermint and marzipan, sugarplums and Christmas pudding and, from deep within the sparkling tree, the dark perfumed breath of snow-covered pine woods, far away.

In Marie's dream she saw Godpapa Drosselmeier coming toward her through the snow—dear Godpapa—so stern and mysterious-looking with his black eye patch and his white wig spun out of glass threads. Marie knew how kind he was in spite of the way he looked. She could tell by the twinkle in his eye when he spoke and the tender way he held her hand when they walked, but she loved him most of all because everything he touched seemed to awaken and come to life.

Each time he came to repair one of the musical clocks in Papa's collection, he would bring Marie and Fritz a small gift. Out of the deep folds of his enormous cape, as if by magic, would appear a tiny doll that danced on the palm of his hand, finishing with a graceful bow, or a rabbit and fox that chased each other in a never ending circle. At Christmastime he gave them a present so special that it would be theirs to play with only on Christmas day. Thereafter it was put into the big cupboard that Papa had built to hold all of Godpapa's inventions.

Suddenly Marie awakened. Some sixth sense told her it was nearly time and their guests would be arriving any minute. She peeked through the keyhole . . . Oh! The final touches were being put on the tree by her father. She quickly shook Fritz to

waken him. Like a genie out of a bottle he was at the keyhole shoving Marie out of the way. Marie fought for another look, they pushed and twisted and pulled and . . . at that moment Mama and Papa entered the parlor.

Luckily for Fritz and Marie, just as they were about to be scolded the first of the guests arrived. Fritz, grinning, streaked away to greet his friends. How dashing the

men were, Marie thought, like cavaliers, and how elegantly the women were dressed, in their flowing capes and gowns, carrying little fur muffs out of which came a chilled fragrance, like flowers that opened at night. Marie's friends twirled out of their coats as they too showed off their splendid holiday dresses. Marie called the girls to a tea party, while the boys played leapfrog. Suddenly the doors opened and they all tumbled inside. The darkened room was lit by pale blue moonlight dancing on new-fallen snow, while candles scattered yellow diamonds everywhere. The children stood in silence. In front of them was the vast tree with its bounty of presents. Delirious with excitement they flew toward it, jumping as high as they could, reaching out as if to hug the tree, while the littlest ones were picked up and held overhead by their parents.

With a clap of Papa's hands the gaslights were turned on and the room filled with a warm golden glow. He called the children to a circle at the foot of the tree and the games began. Marie had been looking forward to this for a whole year. There would be presents and dances and unexpected events, especially when Godpapa Drosselmeier arrived.

Papa now had the boys marching as if they were wooden soldiers while Mama gathered the girls together and, barely able to keep from laughing, urged them to ask

the boys to dance. Fritz dashed to the head of the line and with a sweeping bow offered himself to Marie's best friend. But it was as if he were invisible. She paid no attention to him and danced away on someone else's arm. Then Fritz  bowed deeper and longer to each girl in turn, but no girl would dance with him. Seeing his dilemma, Mama came to his rescue. Fritz gave Marie a dark look filled with splinters. Actually he liked dancing with Mama. He loved the way she glided about and the beautiful way she tilted her head when she looked at him. In a

moment his disappointment passed and he threw himself into the dance with all of his energy. Of course he couldn't stop himself from giving Marie's curls a good yank when he passed her on the floor. Now all the fathers came out and danced with their daughters. They were followed by the boys, who knelt as the girls spun around the room. Everyone was dancing in a long line, swooping under arches of hands held high overhead, when all of a sudden Marie's grandparents and more cousins arrived.

The dance came to a halt while the new-comers took off their snow-covered cloaks and offered frosted, apple-red lips to cheeks now flushed and warm from dancing. Mama gathered all the children around her for a treat of special Turkish delights while Grandpa made

a toast—"Gesundundshtarkundmazeldickundlebensraum"—"To health and strength and luck and room for everyone to live in peace." Grandma and Grandpa were given the seats of honor in the middle of the room and from all around them a steady stream of presents flowed: dolls with petticoats and lacework for the girls; drums, bugles and snappy little shiny hats for the boys. They all raced around the room with the giddy burst of joy that comes when you know Christmas is really here.

At that moment the great owl on the grandfather's clock flapped its wings and

sounded 8 o'clock, WHOOO, WHOOO, WHOOO ... Whose shadow was that grow-

ing longer on the wall behind the clock? The lights in the room shivered and the

children moved to the comfort of their parents' sides. Marie peered from behind her

mother's skirts as out of the shadows a man and boy and three large boxes appeared.

The shadow seemed to melt into a heap of black cloth with a tall and very strange

hat on it. The hat slowly rose up and up and as all eyes followed it, PRESTO! The

bundle of black flew open and there was Godpapa Drosselmeier deep inside. Marie

flew into his arms and was hugged and spun around, curls and petticoats and cape all

whirling in a blur. Sighs of relief came from children and grownups alike.

Drosselmeier greeted his hosts and then brought his young nephew into the center of the room. As Marie watched him come forward a strange feeling came over her. She wanted to turn away but her feet wouldn't move. The boy had golden hair that capped his noble head, and gentle blue eyes shone beneath his serious brow. When Godpapa brought the two together, they looked into each other's eyes for the first time and their hands, outstretched in greeting, touched briefly. Startled, Marie drew back into the security of her mother's arm. Godpapa Drosselmeier saw her reaction and—knowing something about the way things work, including the human heart—pulled out his watch to distract Marie from the anxious ticking of her heart.

Walking to the great owl-eyed clock, he shook his head in dismay. The old clock was off by a few seconds. "Eight o'clock is eight o'clock," he murmured to himself, "not a minute past eight or . . ." With a precise but delicate touch of his hand, time was set right. Marie  and the other children followed him around the room as he greeted everyone there in his old-fashioned and gentlemanly way. Fritz, who wanted some attention from Godpapa for himself, ran and pulled at his coattails so hard that the startled Drosselmeier turned and seeing it was Fritz, barely stopped himself from casting a spell on the boy. All the children began chanting  together, "Magic! Magic! Magic!" With a few tricks Drosselmeier calmed them down. Then with a flourish of his coattails he brought out of two large boxes a pair of life-size dolls: Harlequin and Columbine. Godpapa and his nephew grew serious now; it was clear that the nephew was the magician's apprentice. Placing a hand on each doll's back and slowly turning an invisible key, they brought them to life. Up stood the dolls, eyes wide open, as if out of a long, deep sleep. At first their movements were stiff, but only for a moment; then they whirled about the room in pirouettes and arabesques, sending kisses to everyone. Drosselmeier capered

behind, spinning them faster and faster, giving them directions in a low throaty voice or with a nod of his head. Then, as suddenly as they had started, they stopped and were hurriedly carried back to their boxes.

A low rumble began that gave goose bumps to everyone there. It sounded like a drum roll or distant thunder coming closer. Out of the third box stepped a life-size toy soldier. He marched steadily into the room, jumped high into the air, turned smartly to the right, snapped into a kneeling position, and with a windmill whirling of his arm brought it  sharply level, like a rifle, and POP! All the children fell over back-ward, so convincing was his gesture. Into the air he jumped again! He was under the mastery of his creator, as everyone could see. Drosselmeier whirled him around, marched him up and back, spun him in whizzing circles and then brought him to rest with a perfect salute. This display of power and grace left everyone spellbound.

The children begged Drosselmeier for another treat. Without a moment's hesitation, he turned and brought out a hobby horse whose head was so perfectly carved it belonged on a carousel. All of the children wanted it, but it was Marie to whom the red silk reins were handed. Suddenly, her best friend, Eve, overcome by desire, tore the horse from Marie's arms. Marie was shocked! But before anyone could say a word,

Fritz raced by and snatched the horse from Eve's hands, galloping away around the room to the cheers of all the boys, who followed. Led by Marie, the girls caught up with them and began a fierce tug of war. Much to the boys' surprise, the girls were more than a match for them. They could really pull when they dearly wanted something! Fritz, seeing that all was lost, simply let go of the horse, sending all the girls tumbling heels over heads, as petticoats and patent leather shoes went flying.

While parents soothed injured feelings—and hurt bottoms—Godpapa

Drosselmeier moved stealthily away and slowly drew
from within his great black coat the most remarkable
gift of all. It was a small figure, a soldier from the
looks of him. He had a mighty head, and his powerful jaw had a spry white beard. His eyes were bright
and serious. He held a shining silver sword at his

side. Godpapa turned and, holding the doll high overhead, called the children
around him. No one could imagine what it was, yet everyone yearned to hold it.
Marie was struck by the power of the little man, who was not what you would call
handsome but who touched her heart nevertheless.

The young nephew appeared silently at his uncle's side, holding a basket of giant walnuts. With a wink of Godpapa's eye and a nearly invisible sleight of hand, a walnut appeared in his fingers and from there into the doll's open mouth. With a quick pull on the doll's cape the strong jaw closed and a sharp CRACK! was heard. Out of the doll's jaw came the heart of the nut, which Godpapa held up for all to see. Pretending not to hear their cries of "Me! Me!" he popped the sweet nutmeat into his own mouth. After a few more nuts were cracked, Godpapa presented the doll to Marie. Fritz, fuming out of the group and the Nutcracker out of her high over his head and A moment of horrified out the room. As Fritz  with jealousy, bolted rushed at Marie, tearing hands. He raised the doll smashed it to the ground. silence passed throughwas about to jump on the broken figure, Marie shoved him out of the way and knelt beside it. Her friends gathered around her, crooning their sympathy, as she cradled the Nutcracker in her arms and rocked him gently, side to side.

Godpapa Drosselmeier took out his handkerchief and, tying a sling around the Nutcracker's broken jaw, reassured Marie that the doll could be mended. The girls formed a circle around Marie, cradling their dolls, slowly swaying together. This tender moment did not last long, as the boys, led by Fritz, charged forward, blowing

their trumpets, banging their drums and jumping all over the frightened girls. Papa and several of the fathers rushed in and pulled the boys away. Meanwhile Godpapa had his nephew bring a tiny white wrought-iron bed for the Nutcracker to sleep in. Marie thanked the boy with a long, heartfelt handshake. Godpapa Drosselmeier and Papa winked at each other and called for the dancing to begin. Although all the girls hoped for it, it fell to Marie to have the first dance with Godpapa's nephew. They stood side by side without uttering a word. Then the music began. They bowed and turned and danced intricate, graceful little steps. Never, Marie thought, was dancing so serious and yet so much fun! The men and boys now all brought velvet pillows bearing a red rose for their partner. As Marie slipped the flower on her wrist a wave of happiness came over her. She and the other children, urged on by the clapping of their parents, danced faster and faster, until a case of the giggles brought the dance to an end.

Grandpa yawned, and instantly yawns traveled throughout the room. Marie felt tired but happy. This was the best party ever and she didn't want it to end. Cousins Julia and Elsa were leaving, and Sasha and Christian too. Marie felt a chill come over the room as Godpapa Drosselmeier and his nephew came toward her and Mama.

Little cousin Ariel came up behind her and, hoping to stay, hid under Marie's dress so her father wouldn't find her. Fritz spoiled that plan by brashly pointing to where she was hiding. One by one cousins and uncles and aunts took their leave.

Godpapa, with a gallant gesture, kissed Mama's hand farewell, while his nephew took Marie's outstretched hand in his. The two children lingered for a moment not knowing what to do or say. Then Godpapa and Mama tried to draw them apart. Neither of them could let go of the other's hands or gaze until Godpapa, with a gentle tug, moved his nephew across the now empty, darkened room. Slowly they waved good-bye . . . Good-bye . . . the word lingered on Marie's lips. Her eyes never left his face.

LATER, AS MARIE WAS PUTTING ON HER NIGHT-GOWN, SHE THOUGHT OF THE NUTCRACKER LYING ALONE AND WOUNDED IN THE DARKENED LIVING ROOM. Seeing concern flash across her brow, Mama cradled Marie's face in her hands. She thought she saw her daughter growing up before her eyes. She kissed her cheek and said, "Sweet dreams." Moments later, Marie put on her slippers and light as a whisper flew down the stairs in the now dark and quiet house. Flickering candles lit the big room, casting shadows everywhere. Marie lifted the Nutcracker from his bed and, rocking him in her arms, carried him to the couch, where she fell asleep the moment she lay down. Mama, on her nightly walk through the house, found her on the couch, deep in sleep, cheek to cheek with the Nutcracker. Remembering the sweetness of her own childhood, of sleeping near the tree and being the first to greet Christmas morning, she put her shawl over Marie and sighed a wistful sigh.

No sooner had Mama's candlelight left the room than out of the shadows stepped Godpapa Drosselmeier. Moving like a chill wind across the floor, he found what he was looking for—Marie and the Nutcracker asleep in a beam of moonlight falling on the couch. He took the Nutcracker out of her arms and carried him into the full glow of the moon. Drawing out of his cape a tiny, glinting instrument, he inserted it into the Nutcracker where Fritz had broken him. In a few moments the repairs were done and the Nutcracker was powerful and whole again. Drosselmeier

put him back into Marie's sleeping embrace and kissed her tenderly on her brow. Then, whirling through the room with a gesture that seemed to leave a spell in the air, he melted back into the shadows.

Was she dreaming, or did a faint scratching somewhere deep in the house waken her? Marie slipped down from the couch and tiptoed toward the little bed. Perhaps it was the candles flickering, but she thought the shadows were moving. She felt the hair on the back of her arms rise. Turning toward the big clock, she saw the darkness split open! There on top of the great owl, thrashing his cape and kicking up his heels, was Godpapa Drosselmeier! Marie ran around the tree to the safety of the curtain. As the racing of her heart slowed down, she peered out. The room was silent again, except for that faint scratching. She shivered slightly as she stepped out from behind the curtain. Tiny little clicking sounds whooshed by in the darkness. She spun around to see who made them and was startled by the long shadow of an enormous mouse. Then she felt a cool breath on the

back of her neck. Turning, she faced a fat gray mouse, bigger than she was! Mice were coming into the room from all sides. Marie boldly crept up behind two of them and gave them each a little bop on the head. Frightened, they squeaked and jumped in the air—she was sure she heard them say "Eek!" when they saw her. She was quickly surrounded by a circle of spinning, squealing mice whose long tails, whizzing across the floor, made her jump higher and higher. Seeing an opening in the steadily closing circle, Marie dashed through it and leaped onto the couch, where she buried her head in her hands.

When the pounding in her ears stopped, she realized that something strange was happening. She had some difficulty getting off the couch; the floor seemed a long way down. As she walked over to the tree, it appeared to be growing. It was growing fast! The tree rocketed up into the high, dark reaches of the room, leaving behind a trail of blazing lights and garlands of tinsel streaming upward into the darkness. She looked about the room and gasped in surprise. The toys in the cupboard had grown as big as she was! The soldiers, the drummer bunny and . . . suddenly she remembered the Nutcracker in his bed and ran to bring him near her. In the distance she heard a chorus of squeaking voices.

Fearing what that might mean she turned to pick up the Nutcracker, only to find the little bed now grown to the size of her own. In it, life-size and fast asleep, was the Nutcracker, his shining sword by his side.

A mouse crept into the room. The toy sentry stepped out of the guard box and fired a warning shot that sent the mouse scurrying off. More mice came back in squealing hordes. Marie tried without success to waken the Nutcracker. Keeping her wits about her she quickly called for the soldiers in the cupboard to come out. Rank after rank they came and met the mice head on. Though she was an able commander, the giant mice overpowered many of the soldiers and carried others

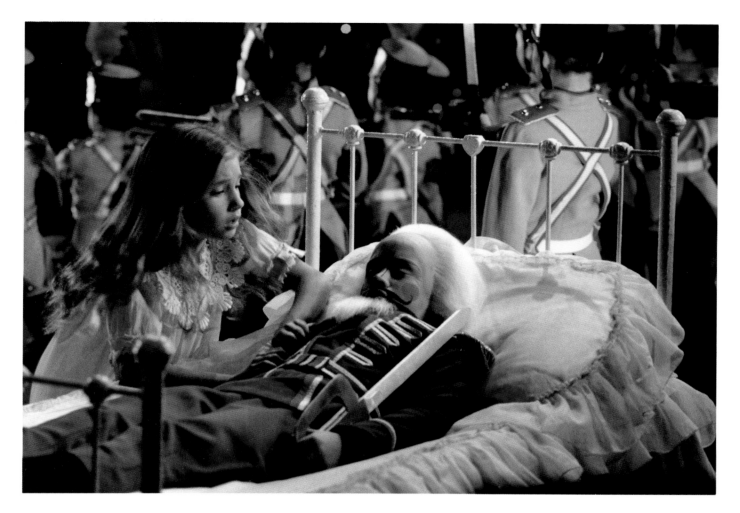

away. Marie cried, "Oh Nutcracker, we need you now!" As she stroked his head she thought she saw a flicker of movement on his face. It was true! He was awake! Hurling himself off the bed, he charged into battle. The fight surged back and forth across the room. Seeing that the mice had the advantage of size, the Nutcracker wheeled out the great Cannon Fondue, loaded it with an enormous ball of cheese and fired a shot into their ranks. The blast was so great that all the toy soldiers fell over backward, while the mice ran around greedily picking up chunks of cheese. The soldiers rallied, charged the mice and turned the battle in their favor. At that moment a screech was heard that made Marie's blood run cold and goose bumps stand

up on her arms. Tearing out of the darkness came a giant mouse with seven heads, each wearing a crown. All seven mouths howled, all fourteen black eyes glinted with rage and whiskers everywhere threw a tantrum on his faces. In his long-nailed paw he carried a giant sword that flashed like lightning. The Nutcracker fearlessly raced across the room and leaped upon the Mouse King's back. The angered King shrieked, spun around and tried to shake the brave soldier off. Finally the

Nutcracker fell. Standing over him, the King attacked him with blow after blow of his craggy sword. Although he warded off every thrust, the valiant fighter was beginning to tire. Out from behind the sentry box where she had been hiding crept the little drummer bunny. Gathering all of her courage, she tiptoed straight for the Mouse King. What could she have been thinking? She grabbed the King's enormous tail and with all of her strength lifted it up and gave it a sharp yank! The Mouse King's seven heads roared with anger. Who dared to play with Mouse King's tail? As he turned his attention to the courageous bunny, the King gave the Nutcracker the split-second rest he needed. Leaping to his feet, he again clashed swords with the King. Once more the Nutcracker fell beneath the towering mouse. He held his sword and his honor high, but he could not last for much longer.

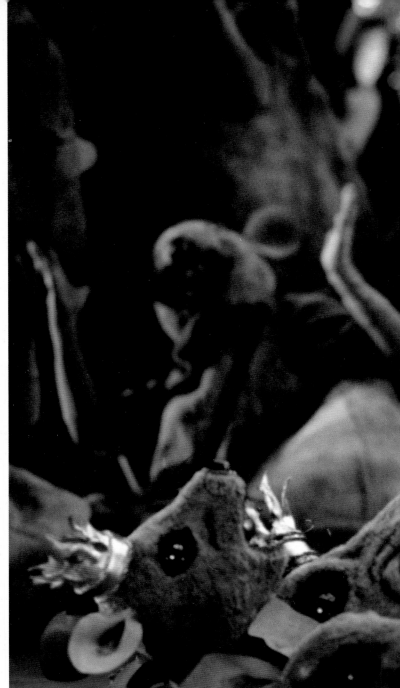

From the other side of the room Marie desperately looked for a way to help the embattled Nutcracker. The cheers of the mice drowned out her voice. Frustrated and furious, she ran a few steps, pulled off her slipper and threw it with all her might toward the Mouse King. It sailed across the room as straight and swift as a dart. A perfect hit! It bopped the King right on the head–head–head. The King forgot about the Nutcracker and raced after Marie, who climbed on the big white bed. As the King reached her and raised his arm to strike, Marie fainted.

What happened next returned things to their natural order. The Nutcracker, saved by Marie's brave act, caught up with the King and delivered the fatal blow before the King could strike Marie. The Mouse King staggered backward and with an enormous crash fell to the floor, amid the tearful cries of his troops. The Nutcracker knelt by the great cluster of heads. Looking down at the Mouse King with a mixture of gentleness and firmness, he cut off the seventh and largest crown. He carried it to where Marie lay and waved it triumphantly overhead. Then he turned and beckoned the bed to follow him. The great windowed doors of the room opened onto a scene lit by moonbeams and starlight. Slowly, the bed carrying Marie, led by the Nutcracker, disappeared into the night.

Moonlight guided them on a shining path around the sleeping town and over snow-covered hills. They flew over a wooden bridge spanning an ink-black river, where black swans, gliding silently, watched them pass. Soon they entered a dark and majestic forest of towering pine trees. There, in a rising mist, deep in the heart of the forest, the Nutcracker walked the magic circle that had long awaited his step, reciting the ancient command:

THREE TIMES CIRCLE THE BED,

THE SEVENTH CROWN HELD OVERHEAD.

On the third and last round the massive head, the breastplate and the heavy leg-

gings that had held the Nutcracker together shattered into thousands of tiny pieces and melted away into the night. Out stepped a young Prince who had long been held captive inside the form of the Nutcracker.

A light snow began to fall. The Prince knelt, facing Marie's bed. With the same gentleness she had shown him when she rocked him in her arms, he wakened her and placed the Seventh Crown upon her head. Together they walked deeper into the forest, guided by the Christmas Star, on their way to the Prince's palace. The falling snow would cover all traces of their journey. As a gentle breeze blew in the secret glen, the snowflakes began to dance.

NGELS CARRIED THE NEWS TO THE LAND OF SWEETS THAT THE YOUNG PRINCE WAS FINALLY COMING HOME. Gliding around the Sugarplum Fairy, the angels sang a joyous song as she summoned to the Palace of Pleasures all the Delights that the Prince and his guest might enjoy. One by one they came.

The first to arrive  was Spanish Hot Chocolate, followed by dark and exotic Arabian Coffee. Then a box of tin-gling Chinese Tea appeared. Candy Canes came leaping and dancing, chased by marzipan shep- herd girls and roly- poly Polichinelles of tangy ginger. Last but always welcome came Dewdrop and her garlands of long-stemmed Flowers that filled the candied palace with fragrance and color. The Sugarplum Fairy assembled everyone in folds of welcome, as the Prince and Marie arrived in the Land of Sweets.

The Prince, accepting the hero's salute, bowed to the Sugarplum Fairy and introduced Marie, who nearly forgot her good manners, so astonished was she by the beauty of the palace. This must be what it is like, she thought, to be inside one of Godpapa's inventions. Bowing before the Sugarplum Fairy, she received a look of

kindness that would warm her for all of her days.

The Prince stepped forward. Drawing images in the air, he silently enacted the story of his awakening. He described the fearful battle between the mice and the toy soldiers. He showed how the giant cannon exploded a ball of cheese over the heads of the mice and how they scurried after the tasty pieces, forgetting all about the battle. Then he showed how the little drummer bunny's courage saved him from the crushing blows of the Mouse King's sword and how Marie's brave act and her little satin slipper saved his life. He described the defeat of the Mouse King and the removal of the magic Seventh Crown, which broke the spell that had held him captive and had prevented him from coming home.

In celebration of his return, the Sugarplum Fairy had the Throne of Delight brought out. The Prince and Marie were seated in front of an astounding arrangement of layered cakes, ice cream sundaes and chocolate bonbons. As a hush fell over the room sounds of distant music could be heard. Spanish Gypsies suddenly appeared. Dark as chocolate and lively as pepper, they bounded onto the stage and danced with fiery passion.

The tingling sound of finger cymbals announced
enchanting Arabian Coffee.

Two Mandarin ladies presented a magic box to the Prince,
out of which flew impish Chinese Tea.

Peppermint Candy Canes, with tinkling bells and colorful hoops,

whirled and leaped for the Prince and Marie.

Marzipan, with her golden panpipe and four shepherd girls,
gamboled about the room.

*Gigantic Mother Ginger swayed
in front of the throne, while from her
enormous skirts sprang eight Polichinelles
to dance a zany dance.*

Dewdrop fluttered over her garden of Flowers
and brought them all to life.

As the Flowers settled into a bouquet after their lovely dance, the great chamber grew dark. The grand filigree ceiling opened to the night sky and starlight scattered lightly over the room. Out of the darkness danced the Sugarplum Fairy on the arm of her Cavalier. With the slightest nod of their heads they acknowledged the Prince and Marie. Marie again felt that rush of kindness she had experienced before. The Sugarplum Fairy and the Cavalier flew gracefully about the room. She was swept low, nearly touching the floor, then lifted high overhead, arched like a rainbow. The Cavalier carried her around the room as streamers of moonlight flowed from her hair. Coming to rest in front of Marie, the Sugarplum Fairy stood high on one toe and with outstretched arms and legs, took the shape of the Evening Star and glided effortlessly toward the Cavalier, and together they whirled away. Marie, holding the Prince's hand, wished for this dance to go on forever. But alas, the spinning ceased as the Sugarplum Fairy, like a rose heavy with dew, reclined into the Cavalier's waiting arms. Silence came over the room.

Then, with a wave of her sparkling wand, the Sugarplum Fairy assembled all the Delights and together they danced a last dance of joyous celebration. As a faint pink light began to steal into the blue of the room, the Sugarplum Fairy invited the Prince and Marie down from their throne. Drawing them near, she praised them for their goodness and courage. The Prince bowed and, taking the Sugarplum

Fairy's hand, kissed it farewell. Marie could feel hot tears beginning to rise as the

Sugarplum Fairy took her cheeks in both hands, kissed her upturned face and whis-

pered in her ear something that she would never forget.

Then the Sugarplum Fairy turned the two young travelers around and ushered

them to her waiting sleigh. Two powerful white reindeer pawed the ground

in restless anticipation of their journey. Marie sank into the soft crimson velvet

cushions of the sleigh. With a mighty leap the reindeer carried the sleigh up past

all those gathered there and
out into the night sky. Flying
into the cool, moonlit brilliance
of the night, with the Prince at
her side, Marie looked down at
the enchanted palace, which

grew smaller every moment, and slowly waved good-bye, good-bye. *The End*

The photographs in this book were made during
the production of the motion picture version of *George Balanchine's The Nutcracker*,
PERFORMED BY NEW YORK CITY BALLET
MUSIC BY PETER ILYICH TCHAIKOVSKY, CHOREOGRAPHY BY GEORGE BALANCHINE,
SCENERY BY ROUBEN TER-ARUTUNIAN.

Film Credits

Costumes Designed by Karinska
Edited by Girish Bhargava
Director of Photography: Ralf Bode, A.S.C.
Line Producer: Catherine Tatge
Staged for Film by Peter Martins
Produced by Robert A. Krasnow and Robert Hurwitz

Based on a Story by E.T.A. Hoffmann
Lighting Designed by Alan Adelman
Coordinating Producer: Merrill Brockway
For The George Balanchine Trust: Barbara Horgan
Executive Producer: Arnon Milchan
Directed by Emile Ardolino

With Children from the School of American Ballet

ACT 1

Dr. Stahlbaum
Robert LaFosse

Frau Stahlbaum
Heather Watts

THEIR CHILDREN
Marie
Jessica Lynn Cohen
Fritz
Peter Reznick

THE GUESTS
Parents
Heléne Alexopoulos
Lauren Hauser
Melinda Roy
Stephanie Saland
Simone Schumacher
Deborah Wingert
Lindsay Fischer
Kipling Houston
Peter Naumann
Alexandre Proia
Jock Soto
Erlends Zieminch
Children
Kimberly Cortes
Eve Harrison
Petra Hoerrner
Miriam Peterson
Ashley Siebert
Kielley Young
Misha Braun
Alexander Levine
Igor Odessky
Andrei Vitoptov
Alex Wiesendanger
Teenagers
Priscilla Pellecchia
Robert Wersinger
Grandparents
Karin von Aroldingen
Edward Bigelow

The Maids
Zippora Karz
Julie Michael

Herr Drosselmeier
Bart Robinson Cook

His Nephew (The Nutcracker)
Macaulay Culkin

TOYS
Harlequin and Columbine
Katrina Killian
Roma Sosenko
Soldier
Michael Byars

Mouse King
Robert Lyon

Mice
Christopher Boehmer
James Fayette
Espen Giljane
Arch Higgins
Jerome Kipper
Richard Marsden
Bruce Padgett
Todd Williams
Kira Boesch
Sarah Brodsky
Alexis Doktor
Alexander Levine
Igor Odessky
Marina Squerciati
Andrei Vitoptov
Halley Zien

Soldiers
Jennifer Barton
Vivian Chin
Kimberly Cortes
Katherine Daines
Lauren D'Avella
Dana Genshaft
Jessica Goodrich
Danielle Gordon
Brynn Jinnett
Scarlett Johnson
Glenn Keenan
Sarah Mendell
Abigail Mentzer
Annie Ostrager
Rachel Paukman

Miriam Peterson
Jenny Raim
Diana Townsend-Butterworth
Zoe Zien

Snowflakes
Emily Coates
Wendy Drapala
Elizabeth Drucker
Amanda Edge
Michele Gifford
Pauline Golbin
Dena Kinstlinger
Margo Krody
Anna Liceica
Andrea Long
Zoe Mackler
Deanna McBrearty
Catherine Ryan
Pascale van Kipnis
Elizabeth Walker
Miranda Weese

ACT 2

The Sugarplum Fairy
Darci Kistler

Her Cavalier
Damian Woetzel

The Little Princess
Jessica Lynn Cohen

The Little Prince
Macaulay Culkin

Angels
Kimberly Cortes
Jessica Goodrich
Danielle Gordon
Eve Harrison
Petra Hoerrner
Sarah Mendell
Abigail Mentzer
Annie Ostrager
Rachel Paukman
Ashley Siebert
Kielley Young
Zoe Zien

Hot Chocolate
Lourdes Lopez and Nilas Martins
WITH
Janey McGeary
Sabrina Pillars
Teresa Reyes
Santhe Tsetsilas
Albert Evans
Russell Kaiser
Gordon Stevens
Runsheng Ying

Coffee
Wendy Whelan

Tea
Gen Horiuchi
WITH
Miriam Mahdaviani
Inmaculada Velez

Candy Canes
Tom Gold
WITH
Alexandra Ansanelli
Ellen Barr
Natalia Boesch
Charnie Carter
Tatiana Grigorenko
Scheherazade Madan
Priscilla Pellecchia
Carrie Lee Riggins

Marzipan
Margaret Tracey

Shepherdesses
Yvonne Borree
Jennifer Fuchs
Isabel Kimmel
Jennifer Tinsley

Mother Ginger
William Otto

Polichinelles
Kira Boesch
Sarah Brodsky
Alexis Doktor
Dana Genshaft
Brynn Jinnett
Glenn Keenan
Marina Squerciati
Halley Zien

Dewdrop
Kyra Nichols

Flowers
Stacey Calvert and Kathleen Tracey
WITH
Jade Adams
Samantha Allen
Aura Dixon
Tatiana Garcia-Stefanovich
Michele Gifford
Dana Hanson
Lydia Harmsen
Heather Hawk
Romy Karz
Sherri LeBlanc
Monique Meunier
Jenifer Ringer

UNDERSTUDIES
Herr Drosselmeier   Sean Savoye
Party Child   Tagor Valverde
Children Extras   Stamford Ballet Company

Acknowledgments

I wish to thank Pentax Corporation, Konica Film and Fuji Film for their generous support; Bruce Fizzell of

Exhibition Prints for his skill and tireless effort in printing the photographs; Albert Lee, Carol Yaple and Karina Beznicki of

Nonesuch for their assistance; Merrill Brockway, Catherine Tatge and Amy Schatz for their help during the filming of

The Nutcracker; Barbara Horgan, Peter Martins and Bob Krasnow for making my work possible; Louise Fili

and Leah Lococo for their elegant design; Maggie Barrett for her patience, enthusiasm and advice during the whole

process; and, of course, Floyd Yearout for his constant attention to every detail.

J.M.

First Edition

ISBN 0-316-56921-6

Library of Congress Catalog Card Number 93-78629

10 9 8 7 6 5 4 3 2 1

Published simultaneously in Canada by Little, Brown & Company (Canada) Limited

A Floyd Yearout Book

Book design by Louise Fili and Leah Lococo (with the exception of pages 24–25, 48–49 and 80–81, which were

designed by Joel Meyerowitz); copyedited by Toni Rosenberg; production coordinated by Trilogy, Milan;

printed by Mazzucchelli, Milan; bound by Olivotto, Verona.

PRINTED IN ITALY

Elektra Entertainment